SUMMER'S CUP

PENHALIGON'S SCENTED POT-POURRI
OF VERSE AND PROSE

For my Godmother, Sheila Nelson, in loving memory

SUMMER'S CUP

EDITED BY
SHEILA PICKLES

LONDON MCMXCI

INTRODUCTION

Dear Reader,

Since the Middle Ages the best home-makers have known the value of a sweetly scented room – the effect is most appealing and gives an instant welcome. In olden times this was done to disguise the unpleasant odours of a life where washing was a weekly rather than a daily practice, and in the Still Room Elisabethan ladies dried the herbs and flowers they had brought in from the garden, before making them into pot-pourri, pomanders and lavender bags. Pot-pourri is a beautiful medley of dried flowers, herbs and spices blended with rich aromatic oils. Placed in a pretty container, it enhances the quality of its surroundings, imparting a warm harmonious scent redolent of the garden from which it came.

Summer has always been an inspiration to writers through the centuries, and these pages contain a pot-pourri of poetry and prose on the theme of this joyous season. Summer occurs time and again in Shakespeare's sonnets and he even compared his mistress to a summer's day. Keats set his *Ode to a Nightingale* in summer, and Rupert Brooke remembered his home in Grantchester in summertime when he was far away on foreign soil.

Reading through the classics, I have noticed how sensitive many writers are to the seasons. Although Jane Austen mentions them hardly at all, Thomas Hardy starts almost every chapter with the season and a description of the countryside, allowing them to reflect the emotions of his characters.

I have enjoyed choosing my favourite passages about summer for you. Many will be familiar, and I hope that you will find some new ones to inspire you to read on. In any event I hope that my selection pleases you.

Sheila Pickles, London 1991

POT-POURRI

WHEN the herbaceous border is at its peak in the height of summer, I like to pick my favourite blooms to carry the garden through into the house during the dull winter months. I select flowers for their colour, scent and now, since writing *The Language of Flowers*, also for their meaning.

I always start with roses and find that a good deep pink rose such as Zephirine Drouhin retains its colour and has a delicious scent. I also add some cabbage roses, for the abundance of their petals, and damask roses, not only for their aroma but for symbolizing love.

The roses should be picked at mid-day, when the dew has gone, and laid to dry on a garden sieve in the shade. Pick as many as you can spare, for the petals are the basis of the pot-pourri. Also pick some rosebuds. After a week or so add the other flowers that have been hanging up to dry in the meantime – peony heads, delphiniums, pinks, larkspur, cornflowers, Canterbury bells, and my favourite, night-scented stocks. I choose a palette of colours that blend well together and fit in with the decor of my rooms. I also add herbs, in particular lavender and thyme, and eucalyptus leaves for a pale grey-green background.

Gently mix the flowers together in a large bowl. Add a natural fixative such as powdered orrisroot, which will help to prolong the scent of the pot-pourri, followed by a few drops of essential oil such as rose oil or lavender. Place the ingredients in an airtight jar in the dark, turning it gently every few days. After two or three weeks it should be mature and ready to put into a pretty bowl. I like to pick out whole flower-heads of my favourite flowers and place them on top. If the mixture starts to lose its scent after a few months, carefully toss in a few drops of essential oil or pot-pourri reviver to give it a lift. The result is spectacular, and I have roses in my house all winter.

SONNET

SHALL I compare thee to a summer's day?
Thou art more lovely and more temperate.
Rough winds do shake the darling buds of May,
And summer's lease hath all too short a date:
Sometime too hot the eye of heaven shines,
And often is his gold complexion dimm'd;
And every fair from fair some time declines,
By chance, or nature's changing course, untrimm'd;
But thy eternal summer shall not fade
Nor lose possession of that fair thou ow'st;
Nor shall Death brag thou wand'rest in his shade,
When in eternal lines to time thou grow'st.
So long as men can breathe or eyes can see,
So long lives this, and this gives life to thee.

William Shakespeare, 1564-1616

THE PERFUMED GARDEN

THE most exquisite perfume known to my garden is that of the Wallflowers; there is nothing equal to it. They blossom early, and generally before June has passed they are gone, and have left me mourning their too swift departure. I wonder they are not more generally cultivated, but I fancy the fact that they do not blossom till the second year has much to do with their rarity. It requires so much more faith and patience to wait a whole year, and meanwhile carefully watch and tend the plants, excepting during the time when winter covers them with a blanket of snow; but when at last spring comes and the tardy flowers appear, then one is a thousand times repaid for all the tedious months of waiting. They return such wealth of bloom and fragrance for the care and thought bestowed on them! Their thick spikes of velvet blossoms are in all shades of rich red, from scarlet to the darkest brown, from light gold to orange; some are purple; and their odor, – who shall describe it! Violets, Roses, Lilies, Sweet Peas, Mignonette, and Heliotrope, with a dash of Honeysuckle, all mingled in a heavenly whole. There is no perfume which I know that can equal it.

From *An Island Garden* by Celia Thaxter, 1835-1894

An Absent Lover Returns

Molly was sitting in her pretty white invalid's dress, half reading, half dreaming, for the June air was so clear and ambient, the garden so full of bloom, the trees so full of leaf, that reading by the open window was only a pretence at such a time; besides which, Mrs Gibson continually interrupted her with remarks about the pattern of her worsted work. It was after lunch – orthodox calling time, when Maria ushered in Mr Roger Hamley. Molly started up; and then stood shyly and quietly in her place while a bronzed, bearded, grave man came into the room, in whom she at first had to seek for the merry boyish face she knew by heart only two years ago. But months in the climates in which Roger had been travelling age as much as years in more temperate regions. And constant thought and anxiety, while in daily peril of life, deepen the lines of character upon the face. Moreover, the circumstances that had of late affected him personally were not of a nature to make him either buoyant or cheerful. But his voice was the same; that was the first point of the old friend Molly caught, when he addressed her in a tone far softer than he used in speaking conventional politenesses to her step-mother.

'I was so sorry to hear how ill you had been! You are looking but delicate!' letting his eyes rest upon her face with affectionate examination. Molly felt herself colour all over with the consciousness of his regard. To do something to put an end to it, she looked up, and showed him her beautiful soft grey eyes, which he never remembered to have noticed before. She smiled at him as she blushed still deeper, and said:

'Oh! I am quite strong now to what I was. It would be a shame to be ill when everything is in its full summer beauty.'

From *Wives and Daughters* by Elizabeth Gaskell, 1810-1865

ARIEL

WHERE the bee sucks, there suck I;
In a cowslip's bell I lie;
There I couch when owls do cry.
On the bat's back I do fly
After summer merrily.
Merrily, merrily shall I live now
Under the blossom that hangs on the bough.

From *The Tempest*, by William Shakespeare, 1564-1616

RIVER NYMPHS

THERE, in a Meadow, by the Rivers side,
A Flocke of Nymphes I chauncèd to espy,
All lovely Daughters of the Flood thereby,
With goodly greenish locks, all loose untyde,
As each had bene a Bryde;
And each one had a little wicker basket,
Made of the twigs, entraylèd curiously,
In which they gathered flowers to fill their flasket,
And with fine Fingers crept full feateously
The tender stalkes on hye.
Of every sort, which in that Meadow grew,
They gathered some; the Violet, pallid blew,
The little Dazie, that at evening closes,
The virgin Lillie, and the Primrose trew,
With store of vermeil Roses,
To decke their Bridegromes posies
Against the Brydale day, which was not long:
Sweete Themmes! runne softly, till I end my Song.

From *Prothalamion* by Edmund Spenser, 1552?-1599

AN AROMATIC JUNE

THERE had never been such a June in Eagle Country. Usually it was a month of moods, with abrupt alternations of belated frost and midsummer heat; this year, day followed day in a sequence of temperate beauty. Every morning a breeze blew steadily from the hills. Toward noon it built up great canopies of white cloud that threw a cool shadow over fields and woods; then before sunset the clouds dissolved again, and the western light rained its unobstructed brightness on the valley.

On such an afternoon Charity Royall lay on a ridge above a sunlit valley, her face pressed to the earth and the warm currents of the grass running through her. Directly in her line of vision a blackberry branch laid its frail white flowers and blue-green leaves against the sky. Just beyond, a tuft of sweet-fern uncurled between the beaded shoots of the grass, and a small yellow butterfly vibrated over them like a fleck of sunshine. This was all she saw; but she felt, above her and about her, the strong growth of the beeches clothing the ridge, the rounding of pale green cones on countless spruce branches, the push of myriads of sweet-fern fronds in the cracks of the stony slope below the wood, and the crowding shoots of meadowsweet and yellow flags in the pasture beyond. All this bubbling of sap and slipping of sheaths and bursting of calyxes was carried to her on mingled currents of fragrance. Every leaf and bud and blade seemed to contribute its exhalation to the pervading sweetness in which the pungency of pine-sap prevailed over the spice of thyme and the subtle perfume of fern, and all were merged in a moist earth-smell that was like the breath of some huge sun-warmed animal.

From *Summer* by Edith Wharton 1862-1937

ODE TO A NIGHTINGALE

My heart aches, and a drowsy numbness pains
My sense, as though of hemlock I had drunk,
Or emptied some dull opiate to the drains
One minute past, and Lethe-wards had sunk:
'Tis not through envy of thy happy lot,
But being too happy in thy happiness, –
That thou, light-winged Dryad of the trees,
In some melodious plot
Of beechen green, and shadows numberless,
Singest of summer in full-throated ease.

O, for a draught of vintage! that hath been
Cool'd a long age in the deep-delved earth,
Tasting of Flora and the country green,
Dance, and Provençal song, and sunburnt mirth!
O for a beaker full of the warm South,
Full of the true, the blushful Hippocrene,
With beaded bubbles winking at the brim,
And purple-stained mouth;
That I might drink, and leave the world unseen,
And with thee fade away into the forest dim:

John Keats, 1795-1821

In The Lane

MAGGIE had been four days at her aunt Moss's, giving the early June sunshine quite a new brightness in the care-dimmed eyes of that affectionate woman, and making an epoch for her cousins great and small, who were learning her words and actions by heart, as if she had been a transient avatar of perfect wisdom and beauty.

She was standing on the causeway with her aunt and a group of cousins feeding the chickens, at that quiet moment in the life of the farmyard before the afternoon milking-time. The great buildings round the hollow yard were as dreary and tumble-down as ever, but over the old garden-wall the straggling rose-bushes were beginning to toss their summer weight, and the grey wood and old bricks of the house, on its higher level, had a look of sleepy age in the broad afternoon sunlight, that suited the quiescent time. Maggie, with her bonnet over her arm, was smiling down at the hatch of small fluffy chickens, when her aunt exclaimed –

'Goodness me! who is that gentleman coming in at the gate?'

It was a gentleman on a tall bay horse; and the flanks and neck of the horse were streaked black with fast riding. Maggie felt a beating at head and heart – horrible as the sudden leaping to life of a savage enemy who had feigned death.

'Who is it, my dear?' said Mrs Moss, seeing in Maggie's face the evidence that she knew.

'It is Mr Stephen Guest,' said Maggie, rather faintly. 'My cousin Lucy's – a gentleman who is very intimate at my cousin's.' . . . .

'Hold the horse, Willy,' said Mrs Moss to the twelve-year-old boy.

'No, thank you,' said Stephen, pulling at the horse's impatiently tossing head. 'I must be going again immediately. I have a message to deliver to you, Miss Tulliver – on private business. May I take the liberty of asking you to walk a few yards with me?'

From *The Mill on the Floss* by George Eliot, 1819-1880

SUMMER SWARM

THE cottage faced south and, in summer, the window and door stood open all day to the sunshine. When the children from the end house passed close by her doorway, as they had to do every time they went beyond their own garden, they would pause a moment to listen to Queenie's old sheep's-head clock ticking.

There was no other sound; for, after she had finished her housework, Queenie was never indoors while the sun shone. If the children had a message for her, they were told to go round to the beehives, and there they would find her, sitting on a low stool with her lace-pillow on her lap, sometimes working and sometimes dozing with her lilac sunbonnet drawn down over her face to shield it from the sun.

Every fine day, throughout the summer, she sat there 'watching the bees'. She was combining duty and pleasure, for, if they swarmed, she was making sure of not losing the swarm; and, if they did not, it was still, as she said, 'a trate' to sit there, feeling the warmth of the sun, smelling the flowers, and watching 'the craturs' go in and out of the hives.

When, at last, the long-looked-for swarm rose into the air, Queenie would seize her coal shovel and iron spoon and follow it over cabbage beds and down pea-stick alleys, her own or, if necessary, other people's, tanging the spoon on the shovel: *Tang-tang-tangety-tang!*

She said it was the law that, if they were not tanged, and they settled beyond her own garden bounds, she would have no further claim to them. Where they settled, they belonged. That would have been a serious loss, especially in early summer, for, as she reminded the children:

> A swarm in May's worth a rick of hay;
> And a swarm in June's worth a silver spoon;

while

> A swarm in July isn't worth a fly.

So she would follow and leave her shovel to mark her claim, then go back home for the straw skep and her long, green veil and sheepskin gloves to protect her face and hands while she hived her swarm.

From *Larkrise to Candleford* by Flora Thompson, 1876-1947

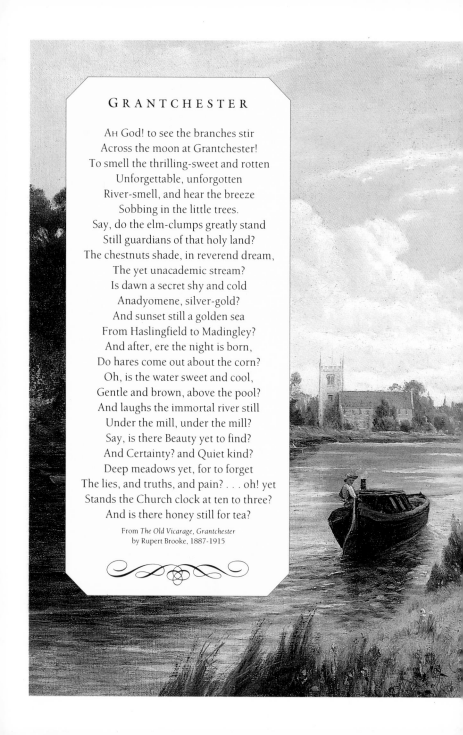

GRANTCHESTER

Ah God! to see the branches stir
Across the moon at Grantchester!
To smell the thrilling-sweet and rotten
Unforgettable, unforgotten
River-smell, and hear the breeze
Sobbing in the little trees.
Say, do the elm-clumps greatly stand
Still guardians of that holy land?
The chestnuts shade, in reverend dream,
The yet unacademic stream?
Is dawn a secret shy and cold
Anadyomene, silver-gold?
And sunset still a golden sea
From Haslingfield to Madingley?
And after, ere the night is born,
Do hares come out about the corn?
Oh, is the water sweet and cool,
Gentle and brown, above the pool?
And laughs the immortal river still
Under the mill, under the mill?
Say, is there Beauty yet to find?
And Certainty? and Quiet kind?
Deep meadows yet, for to forget
The lies, and truths, and pain? . . . oh! yet
Stands the Church clock at ten to three?
And is there honey still for tea?

From *The Old Vicarage, Grantchester*
by Rupert Brooke, 1887-1915

STRAWBERRIES

UNDER a bright midday sun, at almost Midsummer, Mr Woodhouse was safely conveyed in his carriage, with one window down, to partake of this *al-fresco* party: and in one of the most comfortable rooms in the Abbey, especially prepared for him by a fire all the morning, he was happily placed, quite at his ease, ready to talk with pleasure of what had been achieved, and advise everybody to come and sit down, and not to heat themselves . . .

The whole party were assembled, excepting Frank Churchill, who was expected every moment from Richmond; and Mrs Elton, in all her apparatus of happiness, her large bonnet and her basket, was very ready to lead the way in gathering, accepting, or talking. Strawberries, and only strawberries could now be thought or spoken of. 'The best fruit in England – everybody's favourite – always wholesome. These the finest beds and finest sorts. Delightful to gather for one's self – the only way of really enjoying them. Morning decidedly the best time – never tired – every sort good – hautboy infinitely superior – no comparison – the others hardly eatable – hautboys very scarce – Chili preferred – white wood finest flavour of all – price of strawberries in London – abundance about Bristol – Maple Grove – cultivations – beds when to be renewed – gardeners thinking exactly different – no general rule – gardeners never to be put out of their way –

delicious fruit – only too rich to be eaten much of – inferior to cherries – currants more refreshing – only objections to gathering strawberries the stooping – glaring sun – tired to death – could bear it no longer – must go and sit in the shade.' . . .

It was hot; and after walking some time over the gardens in a scattered, dispersed way, scarcely any three together, they insensibly followed one another to the delicious shade of a broad short avenue of limes, which, stretching beyond the garden at an equal distance from the river, seemed the finish of the pleasure grounds. It led to nothing; nothing but a view at the end over a low stone wall with high pillars, which seemed intended, in their erection, to give the appearance of an approach to the house, which never had been there. . . .

It was a sweet view – sweet to the eye and the mind. English verdure, English culture, English comfort, seen under a bright sun, without being oppressive.

From *Emma* by Jane Austen, 1775-1817

TITANIA'S BOWER

I KNOW a bank where the wild thyme blows,
Where oxlips and the nodding violet grows,
Quite over-canopied with luscious woodbine,
With sweet musk-roses, and with eglantine;
There sleeps Titania sometime of the night,
Lull'd in these flowers with dances and delight;
And there the snake throws her enamell'd skin,
Weed wide enough to wrap a fairy in;
And with the juice of this I'll streak her eyes,
And make her full of hateful fantasies.
Take thou some of it, and seek through this grove:
A sweet Athenian lady is in love
With a disdainful youth; anoint his eyes;
But do it when the next thing he espies
May be the lady. Thou shalt know the man
By the Athenian garments he hath on.
Effect it with some care, that he may prove
More fond on her than she upon her love.
And look thou meet me ere the first cock crow.

From *A Midsummer Night's Dream*
by William Shakespeare, 1564-1616

SONG

How sweet I roam'd from field to field,
  And tasted all the summer's pride,
    'Till I the prince of love beheld,
    Who in the sunny beams did glide!

He shew'd me lilies for my hair,
  And blushing roses for my brow;
He led me through his gardens fair,
Where all his golden pleasures grow.

With sweet May dews my wings were wet,
  And Phœbus fir'd my vocal rage;
    He caught me in his silken net,
    And shut me in his golden cage.

He loves to sit and hear me sing,
Then, laughing, sports and plays with me;
  Then stretches out my golden wing,
  And mocks my loss of liberty.

William Blake, 1757-1827

THE LONGEST DAY

LET us quit the leafy arbour,
And the torrent murmuring by;
For the sun is in his harbour,
Weary of the open sky.

Evening now unbinds the fetters
Fashioned by the glowing light;
All that breathe are thankful debtors
To the harbinger of night.

Yet by some grave thoughts attended
Eve renews her calm career;
For the day that now is ended
Is the longest of the year.

Dora! sport, as now thou sportest,
On this platform, light and free;
Take they bliss, while longest, shortest,
Are indifferent to thee!

William Wordsworth, 1770-1850

SUNDAY CONVERSATION

As soon as we had risen from our own meal Mark slipped away, evidently for the purpose of going to his child; and no sooner had I observed this than I became aware his wife had simultaneously vanished. It happened that Miss Ambient and I, both at the same moment, saw the tail of her dress whisk out of a doorway; an incident that led the young lady to smile at me as if I now knew all the secrets of the Ambients. I passed with her into the garden and we sat down on a dear old bench that rested against the west wall of the house. It was a perfect spot for the middle period of a Sunday in June, and its felicity seemed to come partly from an antique sun-dial which, rising in front of us and forming the centre of a small intricate parterre, measured the moments ever so slowly and made them safe for leisure and talk. The garden bloomed in the suffused afternoon, the tall beeches stood still for an example, and, behind and above us, a rose-tree of many seasons, clinging to the faded grain of the brick, expressed the whole character of the scene in a familiar exquisite smell. It struck me as a place to offer genius every favour and sanction – not to bristle with challenges and checks. Miss Ambient asked me if I had enjoyed my walk with her brother and whether we had talked of many things.

'Well, of most things,' I freely allowed, though I remembered we hadn't talked of Miss Ambient.

'And don't you think some of his theories are very peculiar?'

'Oh I guess I agree with them all.' I was very particular, for Miss Ambient's entertainment, to guess.

'Do you think art's everything?' she put to me in a moment.

'In art, of course I do!'

'And do you think beauty's everything?'

'Everything's a big word, which I think we should use as little as possible. But how can we not want beauty?'

From *The Author of Beltraffio* by Henry James, 1843-1916

CATHERINE'S EXCURSION

THE summer shone in full prime; and she took such a taste for this solitary rambling that she often contrived to remain out from breakfast till tea; and then the evenings were spent in recounting her fanciful tales. I did not fear her breaking bounds; because the gates were generally locked, and I thought she would scarcely venture forth alone, if they had stood wide open. Unluckily, my confidence proved misplaced. Catherine came to me, one morning, at eight o'clock, and said she was that day an Arabian merchant, going to cross the Desert with his caravan; and I must give her plenty of provision for herself and beasts: a horse, and three camels, personated by a large hound and a couple of pointers. I got together good store of dainties, and slung them in a basket on one side of the saddle; and she sprang up as gay as a fairy, sheltered by her wide-brimmed hat and gauze veil from the July sun, and trotted off with a merry laugh, mocking my cautious counsel to avoid galloping, and come back early. The naughty thing never made her appearance at tea. One traveller, the hound, being an old dog and fond of its ease, returned; but neither Cathy, nor the pony, nor the two pointers were visible in any direction: I despatched emissaries down this path, and that path, and at last went wandering in search of her myself. There was a labourer working at a fence round a plantation, on the borders of the grounds. I inquired of him if he had seen our young lady.

'I saw her at morn,' he replied: 'she would have me to cut her a hazel switch, and then she leapt her Galloway over the hedge yonder, where it is lowest, and galloped out of sight.'

From *Wuthering Heights* by Emily Brontë, 1815-1848

SUMMER SUN

GREAT is the sun, and wide he goes
Through empty heaven without repose;
And in the blue and glowing days
More thick than rain he showers his rays.

Though closer still the blinds we pull
To keep the shady parlour cool,
Yet he will find a chink or two
To slip his golden fingers through.

The dusty attic spider-clad
He, through the keyhole, maketh glad;
And through the broken edge of tiles,
Into the laddered hayloft smiles.

Meantime his golden face around
He bares to all the garden ground,
And sheds a warm and glittering look
Among the ivy's inmost nook.

Above the hills, along the blue,
Round the bright air with footing true,
To please the child, to paint the rose,
The gardener of the World, he goes.

Robert Louis Stevenson, 1850-1894

A HOT JULY

AMID the oozing fatness and warm ferments of the Froom Vale, at a season when the rush of juices could almost be heard below the hiss of fertilization, it was impossible that the most fanciful love should not grow passionate. The ready bosoms existing there were impregnated by their surroundings.

July passed over their heads, and the Thermidorean weather which came in its wake seemed an effort on the part of Nature to match the state of hearts at Talbothays Dairy. The air of the place, so fresh in the spring and early summer, was stagnant and enervating now. Its heavy scents weighed upon them, and at mid-day the landscape seemed lying in a swoon. Ethiopic scorchings browned the upper slopes of the pastures, but there was still bright green herbage here where the watercourses purled. And as Clare was oppressed by the outward heats, so was he burdened inwardly by waxing fervour of passion for the soft and silent Tess.

The rains having passed the uplands were dry. The wheels of the dairyman's spring cart, as he sped home from market, licked up the pulverized surface of the highway, and were followed by white ribands of dust, as if they had set a thin powder-train on fire. The cows jumped wildly over the five-barred barton-gate, maddened by the gad-fly; Dairyman Crick kept his shirt-sleeves permanently rolled up from Monday to Saturday; open windows had no effect in ventilation without open doors, and in the dairy-garden the blackbirds and thrushes crept about under the currant-bushes, rather in the manner of quadrupeds than of winged creatures. The flies in the kitchen were lazy, teasing, and familiar, crawling about in unwonted places, on the floors, into drawers, and over the backs of the milkmaids' hands. Conversations were concerning sunstroke; while butter-making, and still more butter-keeping, was a despair.

They milked entirely in the meads for coolness and convenience, without driving in the cows. During the day the animals obsequiously followed the shadow of the smallest tree as it moved round the stem with the diurnal roll; and when the milkers came they could hardly stand still for the flies.

On one of these afternoons four or five unmilked cows chanced to stand apart from the general herd, behind the corner of a hedge, among them being Dumpling and Old Pretty, who loved Tess's hands above those of any other maid. When she rose from her stool under a finished cow Angel Clare, who had been observing her for some time, asked her if she would take the aforesaid creatures next. She silently assented, and with her stool at arm's length, and the pail against her knee, went round to where they stood. Soon the sound of Old Pretty's milk fizzing into the pail came through the hedge, and then Angel felt inclined to go round the corner also, to finish off a hard-yielding milcher who had stayed there, he being now as capable of this as the dairyman himself.

From *Tess of the D'Urbervilles* by Thomas Hardy, 1840-1928

A WATER PARTY

WHILE passing through Moulsey lock Harris told me about his maze experience. It took us some time to pass through, as we were the only boat, and it is a big lock. I don't think I ever remember to have seen Moulsey lock, before, with only one boat in it. It is, I suppose, Boulter's not even excepted, the busiest lock on the river.

I have stood and watched it sometimes, when you could not see any water at all, but only a brilliant tangle of bright blazers, and gay caps, and saucy hats, and many-coloured parasols, and silken rugs, and cloaks, and streaming ribbons, and dainty whites; when looking down into the lock from the quay, you might fancy it was a huge box into which flowers of every hue and shade had been thrown pell-mell and lay piled up in a rainbow heap that covered every corner.

On a fine Sunday it presents this appearance nearly all day long, while, up the stream, and down the stream, lie, waiting their turn, outside the gates, long lines of still more boats; and boats are drawing near and passing away, so that the sunny river, from the Palace up to Hampton Church, is dotted and decked with yellow, and blue, and orange, and white, and red, and pink. All the inhabitants of Hampton and Moulsey dress themselves up in boating costume, and come and mooch round the lock with their dogs, and flirt, and smoke, and watch the boats, and altogether, what with the caps and jackets of the men, the pretty coloured dresses of the women, the excited dogs, the moving boats, the white sails, the pleasant landscape, and the sparkling water, it is one of the gayest sights I know of near this dull old London town.

From *Three Men in a Boat* by Jerome K. Jerome, 1859-1927

SUMMER EVENING

CROWS crowd croaking overhead,
Hastening to the woods to bed.
Cooing sits the lonely dove,
Calling home her absent love.
With 'Kirchup! Kirchup!' 'mong the wheats
Partridge distant partridge greets.

Flowers now sleep within their hoods;
Daisies button into buds;
From soiling dew the buttercup
Shuts his golden jewels up;
And the rose and woodbine they
Wait again the smiles of day.

John Clare, 1793-1864

THE LOST BOWER

GREEN the land is where my daily
Steps in jocund childhood played,
Dimpled close with hill and valley,
Dappled very close with shade;
Summer-snow of apple blossoms running
up from glade to glade.

There is one hill I see nearer
In my vision of the rest;
And a little wood seems clearer
As it climbeth from the west,
Sideway from the tree-locked valley, to
the airy upland crest.

Elizabeth Barrett Browning, 1806-1861

Summer Retreat

THE train for Marmion left Boston at four o'clock in the afternoon, and rambled fitfully toward the southern cape, while the shadows grew long in the stony pastures and the slanting light gilded the straggling, shabby woods, and painted the ponds and marshes with yellow gleams. The ripeness of summer lay upon the land, and yet there was nothing in the country Basil Ransom traversed that seemed susceptible of maturity; nothing but the apples in the little tough, dense orchards, which gave a suggestion of sour fruition here and there, and the tall, bright golden-rod at the bottom of the bare stone dykes. There were no fields of yellow grain; only here and there a crop of brown hay. But there was a kind of soft scrubbiness in the landscape, and a sweetness begotten of low horizons, of mild air, with a possibility of summer haze, of unregarded inlets where on August mornings the water must be brightly blue. Ransom had heard that the Cape was the Italy, so to speak, of Massachusetts; it had been described to him as the drowsy Cape, the languid Cape, the Cape not of storms, but of eternal peace.

From *The Bostonians* by Henry James, 1843-1916

A PICNIC BY THE RIVER

Thursday, 28 July

MRS H. drove me to Truro in the pony carriage. Shopping, and then we joined the Truro Hockins and a party of their friends, young people chiefly, for a picnic down the river. We rowed or rather were rowed by boatmen down to Tregothnan, two boatloads of us, the hostess very nervous and fearful lest both boats should go to the bottom. We landed just above Tregothnan and walked up through pretty woods to the beautiful Church of St Michael Pen Kevil, restored by Lord Falmouth at a great expense.

Some of the party waited outside for us in the drive and we walked up to the house, and down the other hill to the boat house, just above which we had tea all across the road completely obstructing the thoroughfare. Our hostess reclined gracefully on her side up the slope of a steep bank and thus enthroned or embedded dispensed tea and *heavy* cake and was most hospitable. The young ladies remarked with severity upon H. and myself for not being sufficiently attentive to their pretty wants. How could we be so inattentive to such fascinating creatures? They suggested it was because we were taking such uncommonly good care of ourselves. Listen to the voice of the Charmers. Is not this a caution to snakes? Charmeth she wisely?

I unhappily mistook butter for cream (Tell it not in Truro) and was much concerned about our hostess lest she roll down the bank into the river. Also I was exceedingly puzzled to find out how it was that she did not so roll, for *what was to hinder it*?

The youngest girl, Agatha, I think, planted herself before me and demanded impetuously and imperiously in a loud voice, 'What do you want?' 'A kiss,' said I mischievously, whereat she flung off in high disdain without a word. But being of a forgiving nature she presently returned and brought me some food.

From *The Diary of the Reverend Francis Kilvert*, 1840-1879

HARVEST SUPPER

WHISH, the wheat falls! Whirl again; ye have had good dinners; give your master and mistress plenty to supply another year. And in truth we did reap well and fairly, through the whole of that afternoon, I not only keeping lead, but keeping the men up to it. We got through a matter of ten acres, ere the sun between the shocks, broke his light on wheaten plumes, then hung his red cloak on the clouds, and fell into grey slumber.

Seeing this we wiped our sickles, and our breasts and foreheads, and soon were on the homeward road, looking forward to good supper.

Of course all the reapers came at night to the harvest-supper, and Parson Bowden to say the grace as well as to help to carve for us. And some help was needed there, I can well assure you; for the reapers had brave appetites, and most of their wives having babies were forced to eat as a duty. Neither failed they of this duty; cut and come again was the order of the evening, as it had been of the day; and I had no time to ask questions, but help meat and ladle gravy.

From *Lorna Doone* by R. D. Blackmore, 1825-1900

A RAINY SEASON

AUGUST 15TH – Cold, cloudy, windy, wet. Here we are, in the midst of the dog-days, clustering merrily round the warm hearth like so many crickets, instead of chirruping in the green fields like that other merry insect the grasshopper; shivering under the influence of the *Jupiter Pluvius* of England, the watery St. Swithin; peering at that scarce personage the sun, when he happens to make his appearance, as intently as astronomers look after a comet, or the common people stare at a balloon; exclaiming against the cold weather, just as we used to exclaim against the warm. 'What a change from last year!' is the first sentence you hear, go where you may. . . .

It keeps us within, to be sure, rather more than is quite agreeable; but then we are at least awake and alive there, and the world out of doors is so much the pleasanter when we can get abroad. Everything does well, except those fastidious bipeds, men and women; corn ripens, grass grows, fruit is plentiful; there is no lack of birds to eat it, and there has not been such a wasp-season these dozen years. My garden wants no watering, and is more beautiful than ever, beating my old rival in that primitive art, the pretty wife of the little mason, out and out. Measured with mine, her flowers are naught. Look at those hollyhocks, like pyramids of roses; those garlands of the convolvulus major of all colours, hanging around that tall pole, like the wreathy hop-bine; those magnificent dusky cloves, breathing of the Spice Islands; those flaunting double dahlias; those splendid scarlet geraniums, and those fierce and warlike flowers the tiger-lilies. Oh, how beautiful they are! Besides, the weather clears sometimes – it has cleared this evening; and here are we, after a merry walk up the hill, almost as quick as in the winter, bounding lightly along the bright green turf of the pleasant common, enticed by the gay shouts of a dozen clear young voices, to linger awhile, and see the boys play at cricket.

From *Our Village* by Mary Russell Mitford, 1787-1855

A MAGICAL EVENING

THAT evening was the evening of the full moon. The garden was an enchanted place where all the flowers seemed white. The lilies, the daphnes, the orange-blossom, the white stocks, the white pinks, the white roses – you could see these as plainly as in the daytime; but the coloured flowers existed only as fragrance.

The three younger women sat on the low wall at the end of the top garden after dinner, Rose a little apart from the others, and watched the enormous moon moving slowly over the place where Shelley had lived his last months just on a hundred years before. The sea quivered along the path of the moon. The stars winked and trembled. The mountains were misty blue outlines, with little clusters of lights shining through from little clusters of homes. In the garden the plants stood quite still, straight and unstirred by the smallest ruffle of air. Through the glass doors the dining-room, with its candle-lit table and brilliant flowers – nasturtiums and marigolds that night – glowed like some magic cave of colour, and the three men smoking round it looked strangely animated figures seen from the silence, the huge cool calm of outside.

Mrs Fisher had gone to the drawing-room and the fire. Scrap and Lotty, their faces upturned to the sky, said very little and in whispers. Rose said nothing. Her face too was upturned. She was looking at the umbrella pine, which had been smitten into something glorious, silhouetted against stars. Every now and then Scrap's eyes lingered on Rose; so did Lotty's. For Rose was lovely. Anywhere at that moment, among all the well-known beauties, she would have been lovely. Nobody could have put her in the shade, blown out her light that evening; she was too evidently shining.

Lotty bent close to Scrap's ear, and whispered. 'Love,' she whispered.

From *The Enchanted April* by Elizabeth von Arnim, 1866-1941

GOBLIN MARKET

MORNING and evening
Maids heard the goblins cry:
"Come buy our orchard fruits,
Come buy, come buy:
Apples and quinces,
Lemons and oranges,
Plump unpecked cherries,
Melons and raspberries,
Bloom-down-cheeked peaches,
Swart-headed mulberries,
Wild free-born cranberries,
Crab-apples, dewberries,
Pine-apples, blackberries,
Apricots, strawberries:–
All ripe together
In summer weather, –
Morns that pass by,
Fair eves that fly;
Come buy, come buy:
Our grapes fresh from the vine,
Pomegranates full and fine,
Dates and sharp bullaces,
Rare pears and greengages,
Damsons and bilberries,
Taste them and try:
Currants and gooseberries,
Bright-fire-like barberries,
Figs to fill your mouth,
Citrons from the South,
Sweet to tongue and sound to eye;
Come buy, come buy."

Christina Rossetti , 1830-1894

Upon Westminster Bridge

Earth has not anything to show more fair:
Dull would he be of soul who could pass by
A sight so touching in its majesty:
This City now doth like a garment wear
The beauty of the morning; silent, bare,
Ships, towers, domes, theatres, and temples lie
Open unto the fields, and to the sky;
All bright and glittering in the smokeless air.
Never did sun more beautifully steep
In his first splendour valley, rock, or hill;
Ne'er saw I, never felt, a calm so deep!
The river glideth at his own sweet will:
Dear God! the very houses seem asleep;
And all that mighty heart is lying still!

William Wordsworth, 1770-1850

A FINE SUMMER MORNING

ON a fine summer morning, when the leaves were warm under the sun, and the more industrious bees abroad, diving into every blue and red cup that could possibly be considered a flower, Anne was sitting at the back window of her mother's portion of the house, measuring out lengths of worsted for a fringed rug that she was making, which lay, about three-quarters finished, beside her. The work, though chromatically brilliant, was tedious: a hearth-rug was a thing which nobody worked at from morning to night; it was taken up and put down; it was in the chair, on the floor, across the hand-rail, under the bed, kicked here, kicked there, rolled away in the closet, brought out again, and so on, more capriciously perhaps than any other home-made article. Nobody was expected to finish a rug within a calculable period, and the wools of the beginning became faded and historical before the end was reached. A sense of this inherent nature of worsted-work rather than idleness led Anne to look rather frequently from the open casement.

Immediately before her was the large, smooth mill-pond, over-full, and intruding into the hedge and into the road. The water, with its flowing leaves and spots of froth, was stealing away, like Time, under the dark arch, to tumble over the great slimy wheel within. On the other side of the mill-pond was an open place called the Cross, because it was three-quarters of one, two lanes and a cattle-drive meeting there. It was the general rendezvous and arena of the surrounding village. Behind this a steep slope rose high into the sky, merging in a wide and open down, now littered with sheep newly shorn. The upland by its height completely sheltered the mill and village from north winds, making summers of springs, reducing winters to autumn temperatures, and permitting myrtle to flourish in the open air.

The heaviness of noon pervaded the scene, and under its influence the sheep had ceased to feed. Nobody was standing at the Cross, the few inhabitants being indoors at their dinner. No human being was on the down, and no human eye or interest but Anne's seemed to be concerned with it. . . . Turning her eyes further she beheld two cavalry soldiers on bulky grey chargers, armed and accoutred throughout, ascending the down at a point to the left where the incline was comparatively easy. The burnished chains, buckles, and plates of their trappings shone like little looking-glasses, and the blue, red, and white about them was unsubdued by weather or wear.

From *The Trumpet Major* by Thomas Hardy, 1840-1928

LITTLE IDA'S FLOWERS

'My flowers are quite faded,' said little Ida. 'Only yesterday evening they were so pretty, and now they are all drooping! What can be the reason of it?' asked she of the student who was sitting on the sofa, and who was a great favourite with her, because he used to tell her stories, and cut out all sorts of pretty things for her in paper – such as hearts with little ladies dancing in them, flowers, high castles with open doors, etc. 'Why do these flowers look so deplorable?' asked she again, showing him a bouquet of faded flowers.

'Do you not know?' replied the student. 'Your flowers went to a ball last night, and are tired; that is why they all hang their heads.'

'Surely flowers cannot dance!' exclaimed little Ida.

'Of course they can dance! When it is dark, and we have all gone to bed, they jump about as merrily as possible. They have a ball almost every night.'

'May children go to the ball, too?' asked Ida.

'Yes,' said the student; 'daisies and lilies of the valley.'

'And where do the prettiest flowers dance?'

'Have you never been in the large garden in front of the King's beautiful summer palace – the garden so full of flowers? Surely you remember the swans that come swimming up to you, when you throw them crumbs of bread? There you may imagine they have splendid balls.'

From *Fairy Tales* by Hans Christian Andersen, 1805-1875

ACKNOWLEDGEMENTS

Bridgeman Art Library:
p3 Maoliid/Joseph Mensing Gallery, Hamm-Rhynern; p5 Ethel Walker/Bradford Art Galleries & Museums; p9 Dante Gabriel Rossetti/Guildhall Art Gallery, London; p14 Maud Tindal Atkinson/ Maas Gallery, London; p15 John William Waterhouse/Christie's, London; p18 Eleanor Fortesque-Brickdale/City of Bristol Museum & Art Gallery; p19 Cassels Book Birds/Private Collection; p27 Henry Parker/Eaton Gallery, London; p30 Evelyn De Morgan/ De Morgan Foundation; p31 Tom Lloyd/Chris Beetles Ltd., London; p36 De Sphaera/Biblioteca Estense, Modena; p44/45 Peter Severin Kroyer/Skagens Museum, Denmark; p48 William Linnell/ Wolverhampton Art Gallery; p49 Julien Dupre/Galerie George, London; p55 Edward Reginald Frampton/Mass Gallery, London; p56/57 John Thomas Serres/Private Collection; p61 A.J. Billinghurst/Private Collection; p63 Sir John Everett Millais/Private Collection.

Fine Art Photographic Archive:
p7 Edward Killingworth Johnson; p13 Lucius Rossi; p17 James N. Lee; p21 Ernest Walbourn; p22 Leopold Rivers; p24/25 Allan Mell; p26 Johan Laurentz Jensen; p29 Edward Robert Hughes; p34 Henry H. Emmerson; p37 Jessica Hayllar; p39 Fred Hall; p43 Oliver William; p46 William Kay Blacklock; p47 Edward Riley; p50 A. Templeuve; p53 Delphin Enjolras; p58 Ernest Walbourn.

Lady Lever Gallery, National Museums & Galleries of Merseyside: p41 Edward John Gregory

National Portrait Gallery, London: p59 James Jacques Tissot

Nottingham Castle Museum & Art Gallery:
p42 John Arnesbury Brown

Royal Horticultural Society: p11 Curtis's Botanical Magazine

Tate Gallery: p33 Marcus Stone

Cover: Sir John Everett Millais/Private Collection/Bridgeman Art Library.

SUMMER'S CUP

The endpapers of this book are scented with the heady fragrance of Summer's Cup, which was created by Penhaligon's in 1989. It contains lily and jasmine blended on a bed of roses, reminiscent of a herbaceous border in an English country garden at the height of summer.

The pot-pourri contains dark red roses, peonies, pink and blue delphiniums, dark blue mallow, lavender and juniper berries.

Published in the United States by Harmony Books,
a division of Crown Publishers, Inc.,
201 East 50th Street, New York, New York 10022

Published in Great Britain by Pavilion Books Limited

HARMONY and colophon are trademarks of
Crown Publishers, Inc.

Manufactured in Singapore by Imago

ISBN 0-517-58464-6

10 9 8 7 6 5 4 3 2 1

First American Edition

For more information about Penhaligon's perfumes,
please telephone London (071) 836 2150 or write to:
PENHALIGON'S
41 Wellington Street
Covent Garden
London WC2